How to Protect Your Home and Life Savings in Maryland

GREGORY P. JIMENO

ATTORNEY AT LAW

WORD ASSOCIATION PUBLISHERS
www.wordassociation.com
1.800.827.7903

Printed in the United States of America.

ISBN: 978-1-63385-342-3

Designed and published by

Word Association Publishers
205 Fifth Avenue
Tarentum, Pennsylvania 15084

www.wordassociation.com

1.800.827.7903

DISCLAIMER

THIS BOOK IS NOT LEGAL ADVICE

Please understand that the information in this book is not intended to be legal advice. I do not represent you and, thus, I am not your lawyer until we enter into a written fee agreement. I can lay out the basics of estate planning and asset protection in Maryland but you should not construe anything in this book to be legal advice about your situation. Each personal and family circumstance is different, and an attorney can only give quality legal advice when he or she understands the unique circumstances as they apply to your situation. You should consult with an attorney to discuss your estate plan.

Table of Contents

CHAPTER

1

How Do You Protect Your Assets

& REMAIN IN CONTROL

Protection of assets means different things to different individuals. Some people want to protect their life savings against the high cost of nursing home care. Others want to protect the inheritances of their children or grandchildren if these heirs are too young to manage assets on their own, have credit problems, or are involved in a bad marriage where the inheritance could be distributed to a former son or daughter-in-law. Some people even want to protect their estate against the possibility that after they pass away their spouse will remarry and give all their assets to his or her new spouse, leaving nothing for the children they had together.

Let's look in greater detail at some common scenarios where people would like to protect their assets.

NURSING HOME

70% of senior citizens will at some point personally experience long-term care. Without proper planning, including the use of a trust, the vast majority of your wealth accumulations will be at risk. Under current law, Medicaid will not pay for nursing home care for a single person unless he or she has $2,500 or less in assets. This amount includes all the single person's assets: home, retirement accounts, brokerage accounts, bank accounts, etc. You might ask, "Why are we talking about the requirements for a single person and not a married couple?" Every married person either dies or becomes single after his or her spouse passes away. While the asset limits for married couples are higher, with the potential ability to exclude more assets and qualify for Medicaid, this discussion focuses on the single person limit to highlight the potential need for planning to protect family assets.

The cost of setting up an estate plan is minuscule compared to the risk of doing nothing. Typically, a professionally crafted asset protection plan, which will include a living trust, could cost less than one month of long-term care. Without proper planning, a family needs to be prepared to liquidate their home and life savings to pay for nursing home care.

PROTECTION FOR KIDS, GRANDKIDS, HEIRS

Let's say you have young kids or grandchildren who, if you died today, would not be able to properly manage any portion of an estate that you would like to leave them after your death. There are many reasons why you might not feel comfortable leaving someone a portion of your estate. Your child, grandchild, or another heir might be too young or immature to properly manage his or her inheritance. Hopefully, when we draft an estate plan, it will not take effect for many, many years because you are alive and well. However, it is impossible to determine the exact date that a young heir will be responsible enough to properly manage the inheritance he or she receives.

Other reasons why you might not want to give a gift outright to an heir include the heir spends too much money, or has credit problems, or has judgments against them. In circumstances where your heir has judgments against him or her, the inheritance you leave could go directly to the creditors of that heir. Protection of the inheritance you pass along to an heir is something that most people don't initially think about when considering estate planning.

Upon reflection, however, protection of the heirs' inheritance is something many people feel they need to do. In lieu of just giving your heir a portion of your estate outright, you can create a trust for the benefit of your heir. The trust allows you to set up the rules for how and when money gets distributed to your heir and who is in charge of the distributions. By giving money to a properly drafted trust for the benefit of your heirs, as opposed to giving him or her an outright portion of your estate, the funds in the trust are protected from any creditors they may have, now and in the future. For a young heir, you can protect the money until such time as the person you put in charge of the trust determines that the money should be removed and distributed. This allows for the protection of the money *and* the flexibility to give that money out of the trust when, or if, the heir needs it or is responsible enough to manage it on his or her own.

> **Protection of the inheritance you pass along to an heir is something that most people don't initially think about when considering estate planning.**

BLENDED FAMILY/REMARRIAGE:

From an estate planning perspective, blended families often present unique challenges. For example, let's say that the husband and wife each bring two kids to the marriage, and after their marriage, the husband and wife have two children together. All told, there are six children in the family. In contrast, if a husband and wife did not have children from a prior relationship, the husband and wife typically create an estate plan which provides that upon the death of the first spouse they want the other spouse to receive all of the family's assets. Most estate plans go on to provide that if a person's spouse has predeceased them, they want their kids to inherit their assets. In a blended family like the one we have been discussing, the following question arises: Which of the six children should inherit the assets? Does the husband want to just give his assets to his kids and the kids he had with his predeceased spouse? Is the husband going to include his predeceased spouse's kids in the estate plan? When husband and wife were married, did they create joint estate plans that included all six kids inheriting a portion of their estate? What assurance does the spouse who dies first have that his or her children from the previous relationship will be taken care of following his or her death? Blended family trusts allow proper planning and family harmony.

The situation becomes even more complicated if, after the death of the first spouse, the surviving spouse remarries. Let's say that the husband and wife have two children during the course of their 25-year marriage. The husband passes away and his wife remarries. As we have noted, most spouses leave their entire estate to their surviving spouse. Now, after the death of her husband, the wife gets remarried and creates a new estate plan leaving everything to her new husband upon her death. If the wife dies first, the assets that she inherited from her first husband will all go to her new husband, potentially leaving her children from her first marriage out of her estate.

> **Blended family trusts allow proper planning and family harmony.**

With proper planning, each spouse can create a plan that ensures his or her children are taken care of even if he or she is the first to pass away. For instance, the husband and wife could create a trust during their lifetime whereby they set up assurances that their intended distributions cannot be changed or altered after their death. This type of asset protection planning is particularly helpful for both blended families and remarriage scenarios. If you want to ensure your heirs' inheritances are protected after your death, you need to create an estate plan that cannot be changed or altered following your death.

CHAPTER
2

The Government Has A Plan For You

AND YOU WON'T LIKE IT!

Let's say you decide not to do a proper estate plan. Maybe you are someone who doesn't like dealing with your own mortality (Mother Nature is undefeated, unfortunately) or you don't want to spend the money necessary to do an estate plan. By not planning in advance, you leave all your assets unprotected and you do not have any say in who will manage your assets. Not to worry, the government has a plan set in place just for you. (Don't we all just love it when the government plans for us!) Okay, in truth, you should most definitely worry about the government's plan.

> **Okay, in truth, you should most definitely worry about the government's plan.**

FAILURE TO PLAN PROPERLY CAN PULL FAMILIES APART DURING YOUR LIFETIME

During your lifetime there are two primary planning issues you should address: Who will make medical decisions for you if you can't make them yourself, and who will manage your assets if you can't. If you don't designate someone to make medical decisions in the event of incapacity, Maryland law has a list of people to make such decisions for you. Maryland prioritizes your medical decision makers as follows:

1. Your legal guardian (if one has been appointed)

2. Your spouse

3. Your adult children

4. Your parents

5. Your adult siblings

6. A friend or other relative

Don't get a false sense of security that, if you fail to plan, your healthcare wishes will be carried out in the event of incapacity. While the law might allow someone to make medical decisions for you, it does not tell your family whether you want medical intervention or a feeding tube if your death is imminent. Also, the law allowing someone to make medical decisions on your behalf does not automatically give the person making those decisions access to your protected medical records, nor does the law give your appointed healthcare agent the ability to make mental health decisions on your behalf.

By not choosing a person to take charge of your medical care you are also creating potential conflicts between your loved ones. Let's assume for a moment that you don't have a guardian or a spouse and you need someone to make medical decisions on your behalf. Next in line, according to Maryland law, are your three children. What happens if they can't agree on what type of care you should receive? These types of conflicts can lead to a lifetime of anger and resentment between your children. A dispute like this would force the hospital's patient care advisory committee to step in and determine a course of action.

While there is a law that allows someone to make medical decisions on your behalf if you can't, there is no such law regarding financial decisions. If you have a joint account with your spouse and you become disabled, your spouse would be able to access those funds. What happens, though, if your spouse predeceases you and you are now the sole owner of that account and no longer have the capacity to properly manage your affairs? There is not another owner of the account to step in and access the money. In addition, many people have planned for retirement by using IRAs. By definition, an IRA is an INDIVIDUAL retirement account, meaning there can be no joint ownership and, upon the disability of one spouse, the other spouse cannot access or manage the funds in the account.

> **A dispute like this would force the hospital's patient care advisory committee to step in and determine a course of action.**

If you fail to properly plan for disability, your loved ones would have to turn to the government's plan, which would require them to attempt to become your guardian in a court of law. If you are incapacitated and cannot manage your property and/or are unable to make decisions regarding your health or safety, the court could appoint a guardian to manage your affairs.

In Maryland, a guardianship procedure is intended to be an adversarial process because the person subject to the guardianship loses all power to make his or her own decisions.

A guardianship process begins with someone filing a "Petition for Guardianship" in the Circuit Court where the "alleged disabled person" resides. Next, the court will appoint an attorney to represent the alleged disabled person's interests. The attorney's fee will come out of the bank account of the alleged disabled person, even though he or she did not ask for the appointment of an attorney, and in most guardianship matters the alleged disabled person did not have a hand in selecting his or her attorney.

Another example of Maryland guardianship's adversarial nature is that the alleged disabled person can contest the imposition of guardianship and have his or her case heard before a jury. This means that six people the alleged disabled person has never met would be deciding that person's competence and, if he or she is deemed incompetent, the same six-person jury would also decide who will make financial and medical decisions for the disabled person for the remainder of his or her life.

As you can see, guardianship proceedings can be time-consuming, expensive, and invasive, since every aspect of the alleged disabled person's medical conditions, competency, and finances can be explored during the guardianship proceedings. Properly executed financial and medical powers of attorney, or a living trust, could alleviate the need for a guardianship proceeding.

THE GOVERNMENT'S PLAN CAN PULL FAMILIES APART AFTER YOUR DEATH

Why would you allow the state to choose where your assets are distributed upon your death? Let's say you have three children, but you have always *thought* your oldest child should serve as your personal representative (the person designated to settle your affairs after your death). However, if you don't properly designate your oldest child as your personal representative during your lifetime, each child will likely think that he or she should be your personal representative. The court will then have to determine which one of your children should serve as your personal representative. Without proper planning your family members may be pitted against one another; what a sad and avoidable legacy.

It is entirely possible that the person appointed by the court to serve as your personal representative will be someone you did not want to serve in this capacity.

Once a personal representative is appointed, the next step is to determine who gets the money and property from your estate. Nearly all of the estate plans we have written over the years provide that spouses want to leave everything to one another and the surviving spouse would then leave everything to their children. If you don't plan and set forth where your assets will go after your death, the default distributions that the government mandates will not be where most people would want their money to go.

> **Without proper planning your family members may be pitted against one another; what a sad and avoidable legacy.**

Below are the government-mandated distributions in Maryland should you fail to plan prior to death:

1. Only if there are no surviving children or parents at the time of death will your spouse get your full estate

2. If you are married and have a minor child or children, your surviving spouse will get ONE-HALF of your estate and the remaining one-half will be distributed to the minor children

3. If you are married and have lineal descendants (adult children, grandchildren, and great-grandchildren), your spouse will get the first $40,000 from your estate and one-half of the remainder of your estate, with the other half split between your lineal descendants

4. If you have no children BUT you do have surviving parents, your spouse is entitled to the first $40,000

from your estate and one-half of the remainder of your estate, with the other half split between your surviving parent(s)

It is likely that most people would not want to have their assets distributed according to the above default mandates. As mentioned earlier, spouses typically want to ensure that their surviving spouse is taken care of and can live a comfortable life. The surviving spouse is generally entrusted with determining what he or she needs to live on and can make voluntary gifts to children and others. The government's plan, however, only gives your surviving spouse a little more than one-half of your probate assets after death.

An aging will or estate plan can lead to disastrous results if not changed to reflect current law and survivors. Incomplete or improperly designed plans can be worse than having no plan at all. Let's say you create a will or trust and you leave everything to your surviving spouse. However, you list the beneficiary designations under your IRA accounts as your children. Even though your will or trust reads "Leave everything to my spouse," your IRAs will be given to your kids. What you have listed in your beneficiary designations trumps whatever you have in your will.

Getting estate planning documents from the internet rather than seeking competent legal advice could lead to inconsistencies within your estate plan, which in turn could make your assets vulnerable after your death.

> **What you have listed in your beneficiary designations trumps whatever you have in your will.**

CHAPTER
3

When There Is A Will,

THERE'S A WAY TO DO IT WRONG

HOW DO YOU AVOID PROBATE?

Most people know they should have a will, but not everyone really knows what it is, what it does, and what it doesn't do. A will is a legal document that states what you want done about various issues when you die. Most commonly, it coordinates the distribution of assets titled in your name after your death. A will does not protect your assets during your lifetime or after you pass away.

The instructions in the will tell a person of your choosing, called a "Personal Representative" in Maryland, what to do with your money and your property upon your death. The person who creates a will is called the "testator" while he or she is alive and the "decedent" after death. People who inherit money or property from the decedent are called "beneficiaries".

> **A will does not protect your assets during your lifetime or after you pass away.**

A will is valid only if it is signed by the testator and witnessed by two individuals in the testator's presence. It is legally permissible for beneficiaries to be the witnesses, but not advisable.

Let's say that you have created a valid will. It only provides instructions for the distribution of assets titled in your name when you die. This means that property titled to you and another person does not pass through your will. Consider the following example. If you added your brother's name to your bank account as a co-owner, that account would pass to your brother, not to the beneficiaries you specified in your will, upon your death.

Your will does not automatically control the distribution of life insurance proceeds or retirement accounts. Those pass to the beneficiaries you named in the documents provided by the institutions holding your assets. These beneficiaries may or may not be the same beneficiaries named in your will. The percentages you stipulated for them in the two documents may differ as well.

Clearly, choosing a Personal Representative is an important decision. It is essential to pick someone you can trust to carry out your wishes and accept the burden of guiding your estate through the court system efficiently. Your Personal Representative must navigate the probate process, fulfill all of the court's requirements, pay your bills and taxes with estate assets, distribute your assets to beneficiaries, and more. This means your Personal Representative is part accountant, part landlord, part lawyer, part taxi driver making trips back-and-forth to the courthouse...being the Personal Representative is not an easy job.

It is important to note that a will is valid until superseded by another will. This means that a will, however old and outdated, is still valid, even if it names a former spouse as a beneficiary. A will can also be amended. The amendment is called a "Codicil" and, like the will itself, is potentially valid no matter how old or outdated it is.

As you can see, a will is not a "write it and forget it" document. It is a snapshot in time that might not reflect changes that have taken place over the years. This is why it is important to update your will as your needs and relationships change, and when your beneficiaries' needs change, whether through marriage, divorce, having children, or even the passing of children.

THE PAINFUL PROCESS OF PROBATE

Probate is the judicial process of proving first that a valid will exists, followed by the settling of an estate according to the terms of the will. In Maryland, there are two kinds of probate, administrative probate and judicial probate. Administrative probate is handled by the Register of Wills and addresses wills for which there is no contest to the will's validity. Judicial probate is handled by the Orphan's Court and addresses situations in which litigation is required because the will has been contested. In the latter situation, instead of settling the estate under the terms of the will, the court must first determine if the will is valid and then move on to determining how the estate will be settled.

Probate is a public process. Personal and financial information is not kept secret or treated as confidential. Anyone can visit the courthouse and view the estate file and its contents. This means anyone can see what the decedent owned, the decedent's debts, the people or companies to whom the decedent owes money, the names of all beneficiaries, and more. Obviously, if you want your affairs to remain private, you don't want your estate to go through probate.

The Probate process does not begin with a death, it begins when the Personal Representative opens an estate in the county courthouse where the decedent lived. The total value of the property owned in the decedent's name at the time of his or her death determines whether the estate is a "Regular Estate" (worth more than $50,000) or a "Small Estate" (worth $50,000 or less, or $100,000 if the spouse is the sole heir).

The Personal Representative files a Petition for Probate that asks the court for permission to proceed as the Personal Representative. Once that permission is granted, a notice of the filing is given to all heirs and all named beneficiaries, in case they (or anyone else) wish to file any paperwork themselves, such as a contest to the will.

After the Personal Representative receives what is called the Letters of Administration, he or she has limited legal authority to start acting on behalf of the estate.

If requested, the court can also issue paperwork that allows the Personal Representative to open and retrieve documents from a safety deposit box (like a will or title to property that will be a part of the estate).

An inventory that lists assets owned by the decedent must be filed within three months of the Letters of Administration being issued, and again periodically, about every six months, until the estate is closed. Letters of Administration are open to the public, including any creditors, family members or others who might wish to contest the will's terms. In addition, once the Letters of Administration are issued, the Personal Representative must place a public notice in local newspapers announcing that the estate is legally opened. Creditors are then notified of the estate's existence and have six months to file a claim against the estate for debts owed by the decedent. These debts must be paid from the estate before any money is distributed to the beneficiaries, meaning there is at least a six-month delay for the estate to be settled and for beneficiaries to receive their inheritances.

If a claim is filed contesting the validity of the will, or the capacity of the person who made the will is in question, the litigation process will result in significant legal fees and the delays could be measured in years not months. In such a situation, no assets can be distributed to beneficiaries until the litigation process and any appeals are completed.

Once all of the creditors' claims and taxes are approved, a Petition to close the estate is filed with the court. The Court will then authorize the Personal Representative to distribute the estate's property to creditors for debts, the government for taxes owed, and finally the beneficiaries according to the instructions in the will.

> **Being a Personal Representative in the probate process is not for the faint of heart.**

The Personal Representative is entitled to fees (based on the size of the estate) for his or her services, which are paid by the estate as part of the process of settling the estate. Probate is a laborious process that can be avoidable by the use of a trust. "Being a Personal Representative in the probate process is not for the faint of heart."

CHAPTER
4

Trusts

THE PLANNING TOOL FOR EVERYONE

A trust is a legal entity that holds ownership to property. There are three parties to a trust:

- The Grantor. This is the person who creates the trust, establishes the rules for the trust, and gives property to the trust

- The Trustee. This person administers the trust according to the rules set up by the Grantor

- The Beneficiary. This is the person who will benefit from the property, either during the grantor's lifetime or upon the grantor's death

TESTAMENTARY TRUST

You can create a trust to take effect either during your lifetime or upon your death. Trusts designed to take effect upon your death are called testamentary trusts. A testamentary trust typically takes effect after your will goes through the court's probate process. With a testamentary trust, instead of giving money or property directly to an heir after your death, you designate money or property to be placed into the trust for the benefit of your heir. As the Grantor, you can establish the rules for who is in charge of the testamentary trust and when and how you would like your heir to have either access to the money in the trust or the power to make decisions regarding the trust assets. In this way, a testamentary trust protects the money *for* the heir and *from* the heir. Testamentary trusts are generally used to hold money for minor children or financially irresponsible heirs.

LIVING TRUST

Unlike a testamentary trust, which takes effect at death, a living trust takes effect during your lifetime. A living trust is like a box and, depending on the type of living trust you create, you will place assets such as your house, bank accounts, investment accounts, Certificates of Deposit, etc. into your box. In summary, a living trust can be an asset protection tool.

Living trusts have several advantages over wills. Why? Think of estate planning as a two-act play. The first act of the play involves what happens to our assets while we are alive and the second act of the play involves what happens to our assets after death.

A will only distributes your assets to heirs after your death (and, only after your will goes through the court's probate process). A trust, on the other hand, not only sets forth where your assets go after your death but also sets out the rules for who is in charge of your assets while you are alive, including the selection of someone to manage your assets if you become disabled. Further, you can select someone to supervise the person in charge of your assets and potentially remove that person if they are stealing your assets or not managing your assets properly. These are provisions that can't be written into a power of attorney.

All assets titled in the name of your living trust avoid the court's probate process. A living trust is a private instrument, meaning the terms of your trust remain private and cannot be exposed to the general public. Further, unlike in the court's probate process, the assets in the trust at the time of your death do not need to be disclosed, meaning a disgruntled family member or nosy neighbor cannot go to the courthouse to get a list of your assets.

With a living trust, the distribution of your assets to heirs will be expedited. If you execute a power of attorney during your lifetime, the power of attorney's authority ends at the time of your death. If you only have a will, your personal representative cannot access your bank accounts or other assets until he or she goes to court and is appointed as your personal representative. Your personal representative might not get appointed until weeks, if not months, after your death, meaning nobody would have access to your assets for a significant period of time.

> **Living trusts are flexible and provide several options as you age and become disabled.**

The other primary advantage of a living trust is your ability to select someone to manage the assets in your trust if you become disabled. Your substitute trustee will be able to take full control of the assets in the trust. We often hear stories of people who have the power of attorney over a spouse or parent and spend considerable time fighting with banks and other financial institutions (and the institutions' lawyers) over whether the power of attorney is enforceable. The delay in the review of the power of attorney can often create a financial hardship on the family. When you create a trust and name the person authorized to assume management of trust assets upon your disability, you can remove most, if not all, of the objections a third-party may have when the person you select to manage your assets takes over. Living trusts are flexible and provide several options as you age and become disabled.

TYPES OF LIVING TRUSTS
Revocable or Irrevocable - That is the Question!

There are two types of living trusts, a Revocable Living Trust and an Irrevocable Living Trust.

Revocable living trusts are the most common types of trusts. The reason many people choose revocable living trusts is that the person who creates the trust, the grantor, can maintain full access and control over the items inside of the trust. In fact, with a revocable living trust, you yourself can fill all three trust positions: you can be the grantor who establishes the trust, you can serve as the trustee who manages the trust assets, and you can be the beneficiary, meaning you can benefit from the trust assets while you are alive.

We refer to a revocable living trust as an *open* box trust. The box is open because you can access and use trust assets in the same way you can access and use assets right now. For example, you can buy and sell property, including houses placed in the trust, and you can buy and sell any stocks that are in the trust. As the grantor who establishes the rules for the trust, you can specify when you are to be considered disabled and who will take over the trust upon your disability and death.

With the ability to maintain full use and control of your assets, ease of access to your assets upon your death or disability, and full probate avoidance, a revocable living trust is a dynamic document that helps to protect your assets from unnecessary delay by the courts and provides protection from people who might want to gain access to your assets upon your death or disability.

The other type of living trust is an irrevocable living trust. To get asset protection from an irrevocable trust, the assets you put into the trust cannot be taken out of the trust and put back into your own name. That is, once you title your house or bank accounts into the name of the irrevocable living trust, you cannot title them back into your own name or take money out of the bank account and place it directly into your pocket.

Why, then, would anyone want to create an irrevocable trust? Because whatever property or other assets you place into an irrevocable trust are protected from your future creditors and, if the assets are in the trust for a particular period of time, they are safe from nursing home and long-term care costs. In other words, an irrevocable trust can be an effective planning tool to reduce the impact long-term care costs have on your assets and the devastating effects on families.

> **If your intention is to protect family assets, then an irrevocable trust should be established as soon as possible.**

In certain circumstances, you might be able to be the trustee of your irrevocable living trust to maintain control of the assets, and you might also be able to benefit from the income generated by any asset in the irrevocable trust. Although the grantor of an irrevocable trust would not be able to put assets back into his or her pocket, the grantor could give cash or property out of the trust to kids, grandkids, or others.

For people who chose to do asset protection planning, it is advisable to create two trusts, a revocable AND an irrevocable trust. The irrevocable trust can protect some assets from creditors and nursing home costs. Meanwhile, you can place "liquid" funds for groceries, vacations, living expenses—whatever you wish— into your revocable living trust. If your intention is to protect family assets, then an irrevocable trust should be established as soon as possible.

ESTATE PLANNING OPTIONS CHART

	WILL	Revocable Living Trust	Irrevocable Living Trust
Provide For Distribution of Assets After Death	✔	✔	✔
Avoids Government Probate Process	X	✔	✔
Allows You To Select Who Manages Your Asset If You Become Disabled	X	✔	✔
Provides Asset Protection From Creditors And Nursing Home Costs	X	X	✔

CHAPTER
5

Putting Your Kids' Names On Your Stuff

IS A REALLY BAD IDEA!

We often have clients tell us that their version of estate planning is to just put their kids' names on their bank, brokerage and stock accounts, and title their real estate in their kids' names, while they are alive. The thinking is that if something were to happen to one parent or both parents, their children would be able to easily access the assets and, upon death, the assets would pass directly to the children without the necessity of going through the probate process.

Rarely, however, do people think through the consequences of such an estate plan. From a legal perspective, when you "put a child's name on an account" you are not just granting them access to the account but you are also giving them joint ownership of the account. Why should you care about giving ownership of your account to your kids or other loved ones? Giving joint ownership to a family member, or anyone, actually exposes your assets to their creditors and debtors. This is a common mistake, made by many, that could cause adverse results.

Assume for a moment that you put your oldest child's name on the $50,000 checking account you use to pay your bills, mortgage, groceries, and other daily expenses. Now, let's also assume that your oldest child didn't tell you that he owed $20,000 to his credit card company and the credit card company has sued him for the money owed on the card. The credit card company can use the money in your joint checking account to satisfy the judgment against your son. By "putting your son" on your account, you have, in reality, given your money to your son's creditors. If your intention is to give your money to your children's creditor, putting their name on your property is a perfect way to accomplish it.

There could also be significant tax consequences to giving your kids your assets during the course of your lifetime. Let's say you purchased a home 20 years ago for $100,000. The $100,000 figure becomes known as your tax basis. Today, that house is worth $500,000. If you gave your child your house while you were alive and your child sold the house, your child could be forced to pay taxes on the difference between what the house sold for ($500,000) and what you paid for the house ($100,000), which is known as a capital gains tax. However, if you wait to give your house to your child following your death, your child would get something called a "step-up" in basis. This means your child would acquire the house at its value as of your death, in this case, $500,000. If your child then sold the house on the day she inherited it for $500,000, she would not have to pay any tax on the increase in property value because her tax basis ($500,000) equals the sale price ($500,000). As you can see, there is a significant tax advantage to your children, or other heirs, in inheriting your property after your death as opposed to being given the property during your lifetime.

Giving your property away to your children during the course of your life does not protect your property during your lifetime or after your death. In fact, by giving your kids your assets during your lifetime, or by adding your kids' names to your accounts, you are subjecting your property to your kids' creditors, their bad marriages, or other problems your children may encounter. You could also be creating unnecessary tax liabilities for your kids by giving them your house or other assets during your lifetime.

> **Giving joint ownership to a family member, or anyone, actually exposes your assets to their creditors. This is a common mistake, made by many, that could cause adverse results.**

There are several better alternatives to giving your assets away during your lifetime. As we mentioned earlier, when people add their kids to their accounts they are really trying to ensure their kids have access to the accounts and avoid the court's probate process. However, you can give your kids access to your accounts without giving them an ownership interest by executing a power of attorney or by placing the accounts into a trust and designating your child as a trustee. He or she will then be able to access and manage your assets in the event that you are not able to do so as a result of disability or your death. Probate can also be avoided by properly designating your children as beneficiaries on your accounts or by placing your assets into a trust and directing your trustee to distribute the assets after your death. The examples above show that you can indeed give your kids access to your assets while simultaneously protecting those assets from unnecessary taxation and from your kids' creditors.

CHAPTER

6

7 Out Of 10 People Reading This Will Enter Long-Term Care

HOW WILL YOU PAY FOR IT?

When discussing the protection of assets, most people immediately focus on protecting their assets from nursing home and long-term care costs. There are three ways to pay for nursing home care: pay out of pocket; use long-term care insurance; or apply and qualify for Medicaid. The average cost of nursing home care in Maryland is $10,500 per month (citation www.Genworth.com), although we have heard of patients paying as much as $15,000 per month for nursing home care.

People who have the assets to private pay for nursing home care must decide if they want to pay for their care out of pocket and, potentially, have nothing left to leave their children or other heirs after death. People with long-term care insurance, on the other hand, must understand what the policy provides in terms of length of coverage (two years, three years, etc.) and benefits (how much will be paid to the nursing home each day and whether there is a maximum payout).

Medicaid is the third way to pay for nursing home care. Medicaid can be viewed as long-term care insurance provided by the government. Medicaid should not be confused with Medicare, which is health insurance provided by the government. You must understand that Medicaid is not provided as a matter of right. There are numerous, stringent requirements you must satisfy in order to qualify for Medicaid to cover the cost of nursing home care in Maryland, including:

- You must be a citizen of the United States or have permanent residency status
- You must be a resident of the State of Maryland
- You must be medically qualified to receive nursing home care
- Your income must be less than the cost of care
- Assets must not exceed $126,400 (as of 2019) for a married couple or $2,500 for a single person (including a widow or widower)

For most people applying for Medicaid, it is the asset limit that creates the greatest difficulty in qualifying for benefits. There is a higher asset limit for married couples than a single person applying for Medicaid because the government does not want to impoverish the spouse still living at home. For a married couple, Medicaid will add up the total assets of the couple and divide by two, from which the assets of each spouse are determined. If one-half of the marital assets exceeds $126,400, the spouse in the nursing home will not qualify for Medicaid and will have to use his or her personal assets to pay for nursing home care.

It is important to understand what assets are considered "available" resources to determine if a person qualifies for Medicaid. The general answer is most, if not all assets a person AND his or her spouse have acquired over the course of their lives will be counted by Medicaid as an available resource when applying for Medicaid benefits. Subject to limited exceptions, here is a list of the types of assets that are considered "countable" by Medicaid:

1. Bank accounts

2. Stocks

3. Bonds

4. Mutual Funds

5. IRA/401k/Other retirement accounts, even if there is a penalty for withdrawing

6. Cash value in life insurance policies

7. Motor vehicles

8. Annuities

9. Motor homes

10. Boats

Some exclusions apply to these assets being counted as available resources. For example, if one spouse is in the nursing home but the other spouse continues to reside in the marital home, the home could be excluded as an available resource. Excluding this asset helps you get under the Medicaid asset limit.

Most people are surprised to learn that the amount in their IRA or their spouse's IRA is considered an available resource for Medicaid qualification. IRA accounts are protected from your creditors during your lifetime and are protected from your spouses' creditors if your spouse inherits your IRA. However, because you can "cash out" your IRA accounts (although you may have to pay a penalty and possibly pay more in taxes for doing so), the IRA funds are considered something that is available to you. IRA funds are not exempt from the cost of long-term care.

In certain circumstances Medicaid will permit an applicant to receive benefits without selling his or her house. However, at the time of death, Medicaid will seek to recover the total amount it paid in benefits from the applicant's estate. Don't wait for a crisis because it will happen someday and you will not like the plan that the government has for your home and life savings.

Okay, now that we have established that most assets are vulnerable to the threat of long-term care costs, what can be done to protect them? Some people are not concerned about this and choose to use their own assets to pay for nursing home care. These people are content knowing that if they go into a nursing home, they or their families will need to liquidate their IRAs and bank accounts, and/or sell their homes, in order to pay for care. Ask yourself, are you willing to do that?

> **Don't wait for a crisis because it will happen someday and you will not like the plan that the government has for your home and life savings.**

Other people are interested in protecting their assets from potential long-term care costs. For instance, some of our clients want to ensure that certain assets, such as their house or brokerage accounts, are protected from nursing home costs and could be passed on to their children or other heirs. For these clients, creating an irrevocable, asset protection trust well in advance of needing nursing home care is the ideal solution. By preplanning, you can select which assets to protect and which ones you are comfortable with leaving exposed. Further, a properly designed and implemented plan can allow you to use and control your assets before and after you enter a nursing home while still protecting these assets against the cost of the nursing home.

What happens if you do not plan in advance and you or a family member must enter a nursing home immediately or in the very near future? In that case, we would need to conduct crisis planning, which involves looking at how to appropriately spend down your assets so that their total value falls under the Medicaid limit. Doing this would allow you to qualify for Medicaid while still protecting and saving as many assets as possible. However, by not preplanning and instead waiting for a crisis scenario to develop, you lose the ability to select which assets you would like to protect and potentially limit the amount of assets it is possible to protect. Also, the cost of crisis planning often exceeds the cost of preplanning.

CHAPTER
7

Is Your Estate Plan Ready?

TAKE THE TEST!

Answer the following questions to determine whether your current estate plan provides the protection you need.

DOES YOUR ESTATE PLAN:

- Specifically name someone to make medical decisions on your behalf

    ❑ Yes   ❑ No   ❑ I Don't Know

- Provide detailed instructions as to whether you want medical intervention and/or a feeding tube if death is imminent

    ❑ Yes   ❑ No   ❑ I Don't Know

- Authorize someone to have access to your medical records and speak to your doctor to determine the level of care you need

    ❑ Yes   ❑ No   ❑ I Don't Know

- Allow someone to access your assets, including bank accounts, upon your incapacity

    ❑ Yes   ❑ No   ❑ I Don't Know

- Provide a way for people of your choosing to determine your incapacity so that you don't squander away assets if you become physically or mentally disabled

      ❑ Yes   ❑ No   ❑ I Don't Know

- Provide instructions to a person of your choosing to make financial decisions on your behalf to ensure your assets are used for your care

      ❑ Yes   ❑ No   ❑ I Don't Know

- Provide a way to remove the person in charge of your assets in the event of theft or mismanagement

      ❑ Yes   ❑ No   ❑ I Don't Know

- Protect your assets from nursing home or long-term care costs

      ❑ Yes   ❑ No   ❑ I Don't Know

- Allow your assets to be accessed after your death without getting court approval

      ❑ Yes   ❑ No   ❑ I Don't Know

- Protect against the public disclosure of your assets after your death

  ❏ Yes ❏ No ❏ I Don't Know

- Protect against the public disclosure of your debts after your death

  ❏ Yes ❏ No ❏ I Don't Know

- Make it difficult for someone to contest your estate plan

  ❏ Yes ❏ No ❏ I Don't Know

- Protect the assets you leave to beneficiaries who are not mature enough to properly manage them on their own

  ❏ Yes ❏ No ❏ I Don't Know

- Protect the assets of beneficiaries who have credit problems or who are irresponsible with money

  ❏ Yes ❏ No ❏ I Don't Know

- Offer flexibility to ensure your estate plan can be amended to reflect changes in the law in the event you are unable to make necessary changes yourself

    ❑ Yes ❑ No ❑ I Don't Know

- Provide flexibility to ensure your estate plan can be amended to address changes in family circumstances or the needs of your beneficiaries in the event that you are unable to make those changes yourself

    ❑ Yes ❑ No ❑ I Don't Know

> **If you did not answer "Yes" to at least 5 of these questions, your estate plan does not adequately protect your home and life savings and you should consult with an attorney. You have worked hard to purchase your house and save for retirement, don't let inaction keep you from protecting these assets.**

ABOUT THE AUTHOR

Gregory P. Jimeno is a founder of Chesapeake Wills And Trusts, which is dedicated to estate planning and elder law. Mr. Jimeno began his legal career as an Assistant State's Attorney for Anne Arundel County and has appeared in court and administrative hearings across the State of Maryland, including the Court of Appeal of Maryland, the highest court in the State.

Mr. Jimeno has been named a "Super Lawyer" by Super Lawyers and Baltimore Magazines. In addition, Mr. Jimeno has received a perfect 10/10 rating from the independent ranking service at Avvo.com. The National Trial Lawyers has named Mr. Jimeno one of the Top 100 trial lawyers in Maryland.

Mr. Jimeno is a recognized leader in the Maryland legal community, having been elected to serve as President of the Anne Arundel County Bar Association. He also served a two-year term on the Maryland State Bar Association Board Of Governors. The Governor Of The State Of Maryland appointed Mr. Jimeno to serve on the Anne Arundel County Judicial Nominating Commission, a position he held for 8 years. Mr. Jimeno is frequently asked by financial advisors to speak to their clients about estate planning and asset protection.

Mr. Jimeno has been assisting clients with their estate planning needs for close to 20 years. Mr. Jimeno is a member of the Estate and Trust Law Section of the Maryland State Bar Association and the National Academy of Elder Law Attorneys.

WA